EVERYTHING BREAKING

/ FOR GOOD

YESYES BOOKS PORTLAND

EVERYTHING

BREAKING

MATT HART

HART

POEMS

/FOR GOOD

COVER PHOTO BY ERIKA NJ ALLEN

COVER & INTERIOR DESIGN: ALBAN FISCHER

SPECIAL EARLY EDITION AVAILABLE ONLY

THROUGH YESYES BOOKS AND THE AUTHOR.

ISBN 978-1-936919-66-6

PRINTED IN THE UNITED STATES OF AMERICA

PUBLISHED BY YESYES BOOKS

1614 NE ALBERTA ST

PORTLAND, OR 97211

YESYESBOOKS.COM

KMA SULLIVAN, PUBLISHER

JOANN BALINGIT, ASSISTANT EDITOR

STEVIE EDWARDS, SENIOR EDITOR, BOOK DEVELOPMENT

ALBAN FISCHER, GRAPHIC DESIGNER

COLE HILDEBRAND, SENIOR EDITOR OF OPERATIONS

JILL KOLONGOWSKI, MANAGING EDITOR

BEYZA OZER, EDITOR, SOCIAL MEDIA

AMBER RAMBHAROSE, EDITOR, ART LIFE & INSTAGRAM

CARLY SCHWEPPE, ASSISTANT EDITOR, *VINYL*

PHILLIP B. WILLIAMS, COEDITOR IN CHIEF, *VINYL*

AMIE ZIMMERMAN, EVENTS COORDINATOR

HARI ZIYAD, ASSISTANT EDITOR, *VINYL*

"Everything turns into writing"

—TED BERRIGAN

"breathe deep enough and we are possessed.
breathe again and we will be gone."

—JIM CARROLL

CONTENTS

IN LOVE WITH THE SOUND

It starts with jackhammers
And the good vibrations
are everywhere, though there's not a beach
for a million years, nor any place near
in the fog of here   Been up all night
worrying under haze of beer
and a tender slice of rabbit, a slice
of its stupid and buttery little heart
I ate it up anyway without even a thought
Plainly, I am blown apart   I miss you, too
I miss you a lot—a leap, I realize, leftover
from the rabbit   But now that you're with me
I hear myself telling you that there are people
among us, who feel the need to dismantle
any sweetness, to tear the loving faces
of angels to pieces   Of other people,
they know nothing   They know
only their own reflections mingled
in the mangled inner circle of the party,
and they know exactly their relationship
to every other body in the room   They have
a cocktail in their paws, and it's the newest
greenest one   They present

a revision of oranges and little fishes
or they present a series of arguments
They are at the center   They are
so refrigerator   They are Scylla
and Charybdis   They are taking us
to school   I do not like school
And when they open their vaults,
when they take off their clothes,
the self-consciousness dribbles
out onto the floor with their shoes
I have been in that position too
Yes, it's embarrassing   But I am
in fact embarrassing   Better to be
embarrassing than never to feel
a single thing—   And you are still
intractable with all your righteous love
Let the hating haters fall to their knees
It ends with jackhammers and lions

POEM

The strings come in
The laughter comes in
My arms are open
to all the murderous
possibilities   I am
not a nice man, but
I am not a thunderous
diabolist either
So for now, the laughter
upstairs and the lemons
keep me company
when I walk
to the house
in the forest
with all its lights on
I shouldn't be at the house
I should go on and on
about experience
how I was a pinwheel once
and you were a dog's nose
or a turn on—or both
The phone rings
and it's a recording

I hang up on
I hit the sky to find you
I never find you
It's way too late
when I come down
I will never come down
and I will not walk
the stairs up
to the front door
of that house   I will
wake up and grab
another cold one
and get what I deserve

POISON LIQUID LIQUID

Two phone calls come
I miss or I skip them
It's hard to remember
all the lines before they're written
Time for springing forward
The grass so grown-ass
and green as dumb god's thumbs
Can you believe how impossibly
we're living together
The days tumble on
The hair grows long
And here in the 21st Century
I find myself a demoniac presence
while you, I observe, are already a ghost
reading something juicy
as a tangerine explodes
from your too lovely mouth, saying
what ails me is this poison liquid liquid
I keep drinking, and by "me"
I mean that you mean me, not you,
and by poison liquid liquid
we both mean Diabolical IPA and Romanticism
We mean logic and reason   We mean

the trouble I have most nights
putting sentences together
because I have fallen down the stairs
some enormous number of times and failed
to come to any conclusions
since nothing's so beautiful or surprising
as the spot beyond the lantern
that's hidden by its light,
too bright to see through, too inferno
to rush into   I love these
mysterious entrances and exits,
every single one of them another chance for us
to make a pitch in pitch darkness
for the whole world's affections
It's the final dress rehearsal
and you're not being serious
but I am way too serious
This used to make me normal,
but now it makes me nervous

THE SLIGHTEST LOSS OF ATTENTION

Behind me, Cincinnati
Above me, something pink,
a sky without windows,
an angel's left cheek
Or what we have here,
broken car-parts-of-stars
Voluminous and luminous   I look
at the ceiling any chance I get,
your unimpeachable nerves   I don't get
a lot of chances   So when I do
I write them down on paper
Copies of portraits of images of you,
every second every hour every day
being called   It's a song
I'm always singing   Then a meteor
or a baseball or a kiss hits my lips,
phrases I've stolen
at length from the astronomer
My mouth to your mouth,
the squealing radiator, the one-
legged cricket   No wonder
life is weirder than the pond
in our basement, than the questions

and answers on the standardized dis-
placement test of bald human being
I'm a thief   I'm a liar   I'm the king
of all the lions   You're alive   You're on fire
You're a hawk with all its lights on
I wreck a lot of deer, dear, but I reckon
I don't think much   You uncross
your legs and re-cross them

D=R=U=N=K

Might as well just come out with it:
Hudepohl Amber Lager—the soul
of these poems. In part. Hard to believe,
I know, but the soul is more than beer.
It's also the paint in Agnes' playroom.
And al Qaeda, which I can never figure out
how to spell (though I checked
this time and corrected it here), and more
importantly it's the whole Art Academy of Cincinnati
conflagration. Hold your heads up, brothers and sisters.
You are the brand new futurismos of everything
that matters and meanwhile I'm listening
to The National, Defeater, and Bill Monroe,
which doesn't make any sense at all.
I'm thinking about Libya and how the rebels
seem so impossible. My thinking does nothing.
My thinking is less than a garden that's been
raided by squirrels. Today I looked
at a picture of peas and blueberries
and laughed myself into a tizzy,
a daily occurrence and way too personal
to make a difference to anybody but me,
so I'll spare you the inconvenience

of the backdrop. I wonder though, like,
is it enough that I'm breathing and saying/
writing these things, and that you're breathing
and have choices about whether to listen
or keep reading. Is that meaning in a nut
shell? Am I just nuts? This is drunk.

WHY I AM NOT A PANTHER

Somewhere it's a Friday,
and in Vermont
it is always beautiful weather
whether anybody notices or not.
People are clapping
their little hands at a lecture
both before it begins and later
also after. They are squirrels
in the distance. I am not a panther
because I don't have a tale
to tell you or anyone
about the jungle, but
if I did, I would drink and pass out
on the lawn. We would drink
and pass out on the lawn.
The days would go by
and the days would go on
with a greenness.
I would tell you just how
scary things really are.
But right now I am a creature
of unnameable distance,
the goats singing songs

of interminable swans.
I go home to a wonderful place
but it's only with a phone call.
The people I talk to, the best
in my life. One of them tells me
she is having so much fun
watching a man making a crepe.
"I am watching a man making a crepe,"
she reports, and hearing this I am sure
of the fun on her face.
"Is that interesting?" I ask,
but she is already drifting
and hangs up without me.
Have a drink, I think. Okay.
I drink. We drink.
It is still Friday.
Vermont is still Vermont,
and whether anyone notices
or not, I am not a panther.
I am a father
missing everything.

JOHNNY CASH JOE STRUMMER

Hello, I'm Johnny Cash.
I have just stepped out of a limo.
You should thank me and believe me
because I have written
some really classic American songs.
I myself am a classic American. Sometimes
I ride my bike places and throw F-bombs around
where people can hear them. It's a kind of terror
of the mouth. Mothers cover the ears of their children,
walk away quickly in the other direction.
I am also Joe Strummer. I am not
a classic American, but you can read
all about me and listen to my band The Clash.
I smoke a lot of weed. I drink a lot of Guinness.
I am a dead man, like Johnny Cash.
But I am alive like him as well
And also like him, I have written a lot
of classic songs. "Daddy was a bankrobber,"
I used to sing. I have been planning this
reemergence for ages, but I have been here
all along. Yesterday I was standing
in my front yard with a garden hose
watering the petunias and lilacs

and all manner of geraniums, and people were
confused, wondering how I can be
Johnny Cash and Joe Strummer
and why I'm a dead-alive man
and all that. Well I'll tell you.
First, I'm a fucking classic, like I said,
and classics never die. They're always
alive even out beyond the bodies
strewn in the streets
of all our cities. I see so many bodies
on the streets of our cities, sleeping
in doorways, rolling around
in drainage ditches, pushing
stolen merchandise in stolen shopping carts.
Everywhere I look there's a newspaper
president. Some of them ask me
for change, but I say change is inevitable
or I sing about "a ring of fire"
and everybody calms down and goes
about their business. Second
when I did that duet of Bob Marley's
"Redemption Song," I thought,
this sounds pretty good.
I should make us forever,
so that's what I've done.
And when I talk to the cats

in the alleys or the chickens
in the darkness, they always ask me
to sign their fur and their feathers,
and of course I oblige. I sign them
"Best wishes always,
Johnny Cash Joe Strummer."
And if I ever do disappear
you should really be worried,
because that'll mean something's gone
horribly awry. Something's skipped out
of the deep groove of the planet
and you'd better probably check
the classified ads and the help wanted
posters and the wanted posters
because the Sun's gone out
and Four Horsemen are stirring
the apocalypse.

BLASTED IN THE SOFT AZURE MOUNTAINS

Blasted in the soft azure mountains
of Beer, I walked to the ship shape
on the horizon where I found
a Mayflower blue replica of a pilgrim.
In its pocket was a key to the garage
door I'd been trying to open
since the fountain mist had rusted
the lock and knocked me back
against myself where I found you
this Pacific pearl

TODAY A RAINSTORM CAUGHT ME

Today a rainstorm caught me,
and I still have not recovered
myself with drier blankets
The brown leaves blowing
the names off the trees   And the squirrels
and robins cheering them on, though not

cheering me   Now anxiousness has an owl
by its throat, pill-popped up to high Heaven Hill,
head spinning one hundred eighty degrees,
looking to the future for some news
about the present

which is useless of course   Even I know that   Mean-
while, upstairs Agnes plays with Grace—
the little neighbor girl—not the idea of unmerited
forgiveness in light   The two of them make up
words to no music or to My Fictions
and The Saddest Landscape

Sometimes it's hard to say which,
no matter how hard I pretend to listen
I am no expert at thunder and lightning

I am no expert at eggbirds and ghost-
typing the air to remember a song

Today a rainstorm caught me up
The rain came down, and it still comes down
The rain comes down is all I know

how sometimes life finds me stupid on the porch
with a couple of empty beer bottles,
humming and waiting for god knows what, some
warm weather to calm me, a few minor thoughts
All these days, reasons end somewhere

The water still rolls with an owl in its blood
We reverberate through it very softly

ALL BLOWN UP

The crying rolls over
I am covered in wonder
Exactly in boats as they fall
off the water   What is
a number   The kitchen, the bed
room, the phonebook rolls over
The memories simmer
like a car up on blocks
I need to change the litter box,
the cat as old today as the last one
when she died   Spent hours
and hours on a sentence
for nothing   Gravelly
to gravity, some rap outside
thudding   I'm benignly
swaying and hoping
you'll stay with me   I'm hoping
you'll stay with me
like a cloud up on blocks
We are bewildered or a beachhead
at first   A tooth comes loose
and it anchors the crying
The boats rewind

to the water, and they're
fine   They're fine
with the drugs, but the drugs
are wearing off   I take
a lot more than I usually need
The phonebooks simmer
It's something I remember
Tonight so much harder
than it ever really should be
Kiss and Motley Crüe on tour
together   Kiss and Motley Crüe
on tour without me   The boats
fall off   The crying
rolls over   The looks that kill
are yours for sure   Razor sharp
Covered in thunder   Tooth
comes loose when the drugs
wear off   You've got the looks,
but when it all goes down,
kickstart my heart with a boat
up on blocks   I'll soon be a speaker
in a deep southern state
Shiny new amplifier, shout
at the devil   You wanted
the best, and you got the best,
the hottest band in the world

THE POWER IS WRONG

Cherry pits and stems on the edge
of the kitchen sink. I'm already
baffled how this didn't go my way.
I thought I might write the phrase
"cherry red jeep," because you
told me I should, but instead
I've wound up on the threshold
of some imaginary idyll eating cherries
and looking out the window
at my neighbor not watering his tomatoes.
Dot dot dot. And that I've already spent
three weeks in this state says something
about how reluctant I am to brag
about it, but nothing about why
opening my mouth hurts so much.
Maybe it's the roasted Scotch Bonnets
I downed in a shot, eyes welling up
in the heat, because it's hot and I'm not
feeling so hot. I'm feeling loaned out
to buy a boarded-up house and no plan
to make it better. If you want to see
the body, come and find me
in the grass stain. The concrete

circumstances I can never manage to say
but somehow I manage to say killing
a lot of ripe deer with my teeth, or killing
my best friend for throwing me
in the lake, killing my wife and little girl
because I'm angry. I'm angry about
birds. I'm angry about value. I'm angry
about worm holes and black holes
and drifting off to sleep, and the day-
dreaming dream of never waking up.
Hamlet, Prince of Denmark.
The Whale that swallowed Jonah.
Thales and Heraclitus and Kierkegaard
and Whitehead. Too much and not enough
of everything at once—I wrote that already,
but I don't remember where—maybe
at length the intellectuals will enlighten.
I smile at the thought of their continuing
absence. Oblivion and Jesus. Go
to your monster and never come out.
I eat another cherry and I swallow the pit.
I swallow the stem. I swallow a swallow
through the window I wallow.
Let us be pigs, black mud coursing
through us. Let us take the light
from delight and make it obvious.

I want to swing from murder
to rapture in an instant. Take off
your clothes, delicious young people.
Take off your clothes,
follow me.

/

ON THE RUN

Dogwood nostrums and fertilizer   I flare
when I dash up Manning to beat my heart
                up, legs catching onto me and Agnes
            waving after me   The trees all waving in the breeze

        for attention   I'm sure I'll be back in a matter
of minutes, but one never knows when the world seems ever

        on the brink of not waking up forever,
instead disappearing with its lights out whenever
                I close my eyes a few seconds, so can't see
            the flowering-flowering trees, only smell them,

        or maybe not even that   Chemical green
and exhaust   I don't breathe   a thought, it hits me

        sometimes only it's nothing   I take a right onto
Coral Park, left on Ramona, there's music in my ears
                but I don't know the words   My mind's
            the pulse that's racing   Cento Bingo, young families out

        walking, a blueprint image for some impossible con-
traption   Right onto Boudinot   The trap of getting

stuck in all the constant distraction—
what to say, instead of how to be and contain maybe
                multitudes like Whitman, because tomorrow, I
        have to make sense of that song for a room full

        of freshmen   I don't know if I can do it
Left on Werk, then back to Walt Whitman who gave us, more

        than almost anybody, the noise and joy
and debris of what *is* in a great big voice
                both sloppy and clear, plaintive and lovely, holy
        and low   *That's about it, dummy*, I say to myself, take a left

                on McKinley, and think about the President,
        born in Ohio and assassinated by an anarchist,

        Leon Czolgosz, September 6, 1901, Pan-American
Exposition, Buffalo, New York   McKinley lived on
                for another eight days, then succumbed
        to gangrene—not the gunshots themselves

        Thus concludes my knowledge of our 25th President
but not what I know about anarchist assassins   I barrel

        left again onto Ratterman, where the ground levels
out, then curves right by the house with the invisible

barking   Now the sky in its way is getting dark,
another left onto Lischer, a storm to the west

the direction I'm headed, wind picking up
and a few little raindrops keep falling on my head, they keep

falling   And by the time I get to Epworth
I'm a little under water, so pick up my pace when I hear
                the first thunder   It's almost all uphill
        from here and there's the giant's mansion, sitting back

from the street with its own private forest   I don't
believe in unicorns, but if I did I bet they'd have one   I bet

they'd feed it a lion, which is a story Agnes told me
once   And there were talons in the fire   I get confused
                when I think about "Kubla Khan" but it's a good sort
        of confusion where anything goes with fast thick pants

even sly foxes in purple vests and bowties, with yellow
polka dots, but right now the lightning's on my mind

and my shoes are full of water, slip-slop-slip
as I left again on Montana   Just in case it's not
                apparent I'm making a wobbly circle   You should
        try it, but someday when it's sunny and not so wet and chilly

Left onto Cheviot, then right on Daytona   I'm
speeding and the rain is right up in my face, and I'm spitting back

curses not thinking of anything except home
and drying off, going down to the basement, reading
          pages in a book, but before that seeing Agnes' face
when she sees me like a puddle   Left on Dartmouth,

some weird secret weapon, then left again on Manning
the street where I started, our house on the right, feeling

weirdly euphoric   I'm beaming beneath
the trees and the black sort of sky, as if revived
          upon a table where shocking things happen

I open the back door and slosh into the kitchen,
          everything breaking   exactly as I left it

/

SOME FLOWERS

—for Melanie

I think I don't know much
about what you think,
but sometimes I wonder
if you think I'm thinking
anything at all, or if
you imagine I only imagine
words in such and so an order
to make the sky fall
all black and wonderful
into the mailbox
so when you open it
a hawk flies out
on the tip of your tongue
And well, that's all fine
and good, but this house
isn't really coming apart
at the seams   I'm sorry
I said that   It seems
I just get busy,
and my mind hurts
from loneliness
one minute to the next

or habitual distraction
I'm drinking too much
probably   The lights
should go out, but not
before I tell you
if I had to choose
between you
and the dictionary
I would choose you,
but I would try to
keep you both
I love you
is the only thing
I'm saying

FEELINGS BOTH HOME AND AWAY

Today after mulching the leaves
and running some miles
with a tired-looking smile
on my face
I suddenly, and briefly, had
the urge to explain myself
in terms of my contribution
to the greater good,
which of course I can't do
So instead I told you
how last night at the play
about the famous painter
my favorite part was
the falling dark
of the lights going down
before the play even started
Suddenly consumed
with hundreds of others
and you and Eric and Alice
right next to me, an ending
beginning and everybody
breathing musically, distinctly
indistinctly   Maybe

that's what it's like
disappearing   But then it was the end
and the house lights ruined the feeling
so my research, cut short,
was inconclusive   I woke up
early this morning and started
reading a novel
set in Spain, and now I need to tell
Paige, because I know
she'll want to read it
I feel it's time
to open up the giant
Cesar Vallejo
Collected Poems
and commiserate
and reflect
on the fraudulence
of words, especially
in translation, as jumpy,
disheveled, and blitzed as they are
Our window of opportunity
is the first couple of drinks
After that sex becomes
a terrible distraction
and death becomes
the only thing I can bring myself

to think about   Now the dark
patches and the shadows of trees
Television football and no one home
to stop us   Alabama vs. LSU—
crimson vs. gold on a hundred yards
of green   Roll tide roll
Fighting Tigers

THIS ONE GOES ON REPEAT

The Man never has his heart
in the right place, but he would
like to feel his way through
wrongness, so maybe eventually
his heart can wind up in the right place
if only sometimes, or   Once
upon a Sunday, though the day
doesn't matter, I put
a Defeater song on repeat
and wrote this poem,
because telling you now,
as little as you are,
doesn't mean as much
as it will   Every single
experience should be written
down, so later you can retrieve it
when I'm moss or as fine
as a very sharp knife   I want you
to know you are the beginning
and end of all my love, my silence,
how the sun never stops blowing up
to warm us and keep us

alive until tomorrow
or a long long time,
whichever comes first

DAILY CHORES

The important things
don't just happen by accident
They don't get said
if no one's willing
to go out on a limb
and maybe fall into the waiting
arms of the meadow, but it's so dark
we can't see it   Or it's so light
I can't see you drumming
a cardboard-box-bucket drumset
right next to me yesterday—
perfectly clattery cacophony—
the latter word a word that makes a shape
in one's mouth   Say it,
Cacophony   Your body changes
Your mind moves over the water
And that's really all there is
You are bigger than lightning
And the waves don't dry up
for fear of crashing against me
If this all seems a little abstract
it's because I'm becoming less
fond of the concrete particulars,

the polyp in my throat
won't burst or go away
But it needs to like a dandelion
I think I should do more screaming
about the contented little houses
of this neighborhood
and the tensions well-hidden
inside them, a million secret swells
of violence and affection,
the motion of the jungle
right here in Cincinnati
Last night's dishes
waiting dirty in the sink,
the laundry too dumb
to be surprising

POEM

The sleep won't sleep on my back
reading Shelley. It's one in the morning
when I think a yellow raspberry, or I con-

template the tiger on the lookout
from my driveway, so realize
in an instant I'm my dear
friend's elms. Protons

and ghosts *in the arms of the blast*.
Skyeing and *deathery*—all that.

BLOODBUZZ

The other night,
we we're in the kitchen
as we always are
in the evenings,
and the song came on
the way it always does
lately, and Agnes,
who is five, said,
"When this is over,
will you play it again?
This is my favorite
song, 'Bloodbuzz,
Ohio' by The National,"
just like that,
those words exactly,
with monumental
feeling. The song
had only just begun
and she was
already thinking
about the next time
she would hear it.

Even in the midst of it,
she wanted to hear it
again, to know
we would play it again.

WAVELENGTHS WE GO TO

"Stuck Between Stations"
in my ears   The sound of waves
I am at the borrowed cottage
overlooking the great lake
Michigan   It is July
Agnes is already six
And I have just run six miles
along the beach   One more six
and I could be the Devil's minions
Or I could be at least one of them

       Today's sky a gray-blue
since it stormed all night,
great sheets of lightning and car-
crashing pockets of atmospheric violence
We breathed it in our lungs
to our dreams, sort of sleeping

       But now, standing
on the deck behind the house
and the beach stretching itself,
its heavy face far below me,
I see Agnes in her coral-blue

bathing suit, rocking in sand
on her heels, looking out
at the impossible water, Melanie
and Judy in canvas chairs
right behind her

                    And with one look back,
as if to say, *Is it okay to go in now?*
or maybe to declare it, *Yes!*
I am going in now, I see my daughter—
still so small, even for her age,
against the backdrop
of the lake-giant waves, the sky
and the horizon line—start walking
with purpose into the lake,
into the slosh and vast of it,
as if she might go to the far edge
and then over it, to the place
of sea monsters, the glass dome
of stars

                         which is when
I feel myself becoming
irrationally afraid at seeing her
so fearless, all her weight against the world
we get lost in, so easily/uneasily

a little panic flooding through me
I am holding

                  my breath
until she turns and starts
moving back toward the beach,
and that smile on her face, even from here,
I can feel it, and Melanie up out of her chair
with a towel   Neither one of them
can see me, and I think to call out,
but the lake is too loud
I wave my arms wildly anyway
with all my stupid love
in defiance of the great
distances between us

IN THIS LIGHT

In this light
nothing and nothing
gets by you, but I get
so distracted
that my notice
has been put on notice
for birds and for traffic
For instance,
the constant slap
of the sound of wind
against gutters
gets by me
Grass stain on my hands
from falling down
at the hospital
gets by me   Physics
Sequined dresses
The Olympics get by me
Meanwhile,
the mountains are
so far, only distant,
and some days
I am even making my way

through them
with my pants on,
which is lucky,
though at other junctures
sunflowers and pine tree
needles   and my arms
in full blossom
as you appear
around a corner
kaleidoscopically
The day looking up
between us
pink clouds

LITTLE HOUSE

Walking straight through it—
this sickness
of spirit—I am jumpy
even at the robins
flying over me,
reading *Natural*
Supernaturalism
and not thinking
anything
The joy in my life
here to comfort me
is not here
to comfort me,
is in another state
All night the voices
of old waving ladies,
grassy glossolalia
from the 19th century,
worrying the fearful
worst parts
of my city, tangling
within me my bedroom
of lungs, my refrigerator

of empty   How to take
the sky's blue
and make it paramedic
or come to the conclusion
that all life collapses
upwards
in tribute to the sunflower
O bewildering backyard
I could stare into forever
O potted geraniums
and swing set and lawn,
and little pink birdhouse
we nailed to a maple,
some hundred years old,
some hundred years
and then some,
the hummingbirds wonder
at its door, but never enter
Laura Ingalls-Wilder
is my mantra

MOUNTAIN MAN

The love in this place
might make a person
squirm   Multi-colored
peppercorns, face painted
peacock   Earlier it was
palm mutes and screaming
the boxing ring, which was
also the love   Now it's the wine
This is for real a to-do list
The love in this place
isn't purple, but it's pink
burgers just the way
you like them, the table
piled high with bills and books,
a grocery bag of still wet leaves
that Agnes collected
to make art out of trees
Saturday is nothing,
or it's the pinnacle of sap
Once I was a mountain man,
but it may have been
this morning   I shaved
in intractable three-part

harmony   Now the sun
sets beautifully, and
it's astringent, my face
full of Build-a-Bear and sparkly
plastic princess shit   How
wonderful to run
all the colors together
in holy dissonance,
which is all and forever
and only about clashing
The love in this place
will save us
or it won't

THE UNUSUAL

There is nothing
in the bag, or it's something
sinister, like cancer
The sky is rife with shrapnel
ducks, cherry pits
and starlets' ankles
Those aren't metaphors
They're manifestations
of my fears as they play out
against the backdrop
of my forties   This minute
I'm not even drinking a drop
of rain, so you can take it
or leave it at face value
Something's changing
the ways I make myself
a monster   My friend Russ
writes the greatest show
on Earth and probably also Mars
Who the fuck knows knows   Why
the rock stars won't answer
when I call them
remains a mystery even Woodsy

can't solve, and neither can Smeltz
in her intrepid vivid glory   These days
people call this naming the names,
but I call it reminding myself
I'm not alone with myself
Stacks of paper,
shadows on deck
Soon I will leave
to take Daisy to the vet
It's one of those days
when finally it's cool again
after long months of heat,
FULL-BLAST AC!
Now back to flannel
Feeling blanker than blank
Jammed to the teeth,
but it's nothing you can see

LINES OF WESTWOOD

Later, when it's clear
I'm nearing the finish
of all or any of this,
I'll shove what little's left of it
between the covers
of some book
near here
And there it will stay
until I find it again   In the meantime,
it will call to me from next door
or over yonder   It will scream
until I get back to it
quietly   In my neighbor's
perfect yard
a massive pine tree
nearly keels over
and buries all
the houses
the gardens
the power lines
of Westwood   Watch one
big footed gust, one finger
of an eagle, one marigold petal

send it crashing
into my chest   And yours too
always rising
against the autumn
of one more year
without any major
catastrophe   I am not
tempting fate   I am living
within my means
for the first time in history
The gutters are free
of needles and debris
We look both ways
before crossing
the street   No cars
only shadows   Squirrels
the only engines
Then racing to the STOP sign
and doing what it tells us
Waiting our turn
to keep going

ORANGE NOTEBOOK AND LOVING YOUR PRESENCE

What if I never wrote any of this?

Noisy blue jay   Ice cream truck

Mowing the grass feels right,
right at home

      On Bear's Head with Philip Whalen

Later with Slayer
             I'll think heavy things

Chocolate cake with opera cream
Paul's heady flowers and the maple tree bracing,
supposedly a thunderstorm approaching in the eaves

I could go on
          making lists my whole life
          with or without wings

I keep telling myself

I'm teaching myself
how to better be
attentive to the world
that attentiveness needs
rather than the world
as it stands at attention, e.g.

sweat bee on my elbow
might be transcendental
might be a transcendentalist
if looked at the right way

I should ask Jason Morris
Return to Walt Whitman

Keep a box of ether in my mouth
because it suits me

The feelings go light-up-in-flames
when I let them

I let them
get as close as is the sky to the horizon

Hummingbird humming

        It's the end of Kubla Khan

The wicked witch is dead

        Thanks for being

/

WAVES OF GRAIN

Here we come! Pies in the window!
Corn on the cob! Immigrants! New parents!
Foreclosed homes! Down the stairs a lot
we fall! Twisting the way we do business
in the leaves! We are at the office! We are
on the job! So much jumping, la la la!
Tomato plants climbing the invisible fences!
We look out over the vast expanses! We look
in all our pockets! We balance our checkbooks!
American English, this is the time Now! We come
to you with volume! We come with our shirts off,
pedal to the metal! Cherry blind! Cheery blonde!
Jet fruit! The acres! Let us hold hands!
Let us eat the cool linoleum! It hurts the next morning!
We are always hungover! What a summer!
Engine saliva! Toilet melt! Floods in North Dakota!
Fires in Arizona! What a winter! What an autumn!
It's hard to yelp and not sound pathetic! Difficult beauty!
Spring in the cough syrup! Merrily we roll
our giant trucks into a ball! Leaning and loafing!
Barbaric electric! We are not making light,
and not bearing it either! The silos and igloos!
Our luggage all stowed! Our ringers turned off! Look

at the sky, its display of drunken starlets! Look
at the tavern, its kissable drones! Push-up bras
for everyone! Everyday a house arrest!
All our lives another stroke! Hatchet breath!
Money cake! Grab your rakes! Your ones
and your zeroes! Mission accomplished!
Your tongues on a sandwich! The tattoos!
The piercings! Text your favorite blood type
to all of the above! Roll up your sleeves!
The incredible gay rapture! Join us!
Happy hour! Mon. – Thurs. 4 - 6:30.

RADIANT ACTION

It wasn't a year like any other,
And we weren't the same people
we had always been. At some point
in the past—no one could remember
exactly when—a cumuliform gray weirdness
had settled over everything. Sometimes
it felt like warm snow falling, but at others
it was more like the clank of a giant's
dust rattling through the pine needles
turning all of us orangish-red
against each other. It had been a long time
since we had shaken hands or pressed
our lips together. All the songs
on the radio were ambulances—not as much
sad, as alarming for no good reason,
the sound of babies crying
and the whole town looking for a wolf
in the margins, but only finding
an oddly shaped three-legged shadow
and some teeth, some fur, an indescribable
train whistle blowing in from the sea.
Everything was mean and low to the earth.
No one was happy, so a meeting was convened.

We all had the sense that something
needed fixing, but it wasn't clear what.
Clem thought we needed a new mother-maker,
and that seemed like a good idea until
none of us could figure out how to pay for it,
nor how to support all the scraggly, unwanted
children she'd produce. Lurvy suggested
more target practice, but everyone had already been
shot before the great strangeness
and given their experiences the first time around,
no one was willing to shell out the money
for more permits. A few people, Earl
and Alice among them, objected to the meeting
altogether, claiming that they had been less
miserable beforehand, and that the green
apple harvest was going just fine—that is,
it had been before we'd fired the migrant workers
and gave up bathing as a way to blend
into the dumpster. Finally, someone—was it
Templeton?—got the bright idea to fill a baby rabbit
full of gold glitter and truth serum,
so that every time it coughed
the air became temporarily more impolitic,
if not also metallic. No one could say for sure
why this improved our moods, but it did,
and we weren't complaining. We all went outside

and stood around looking at the stars
for the first time in a long time.
Some of us went home dazzled
but those of us who stayed passed out in the wild,
which was clever, and when we woke up
the rabbit was the size of a small cooling tower.
What this meant wasn't easy to say.
Adelaide thought it might be a symbolic gesture,
and Horace felt certain that it had to be a saint.
These interpretations went on for several days,
a big long list of opinions and voices,
but ultimately, since no one was certain
what to make of it, we decided to end it
and end it definitively—end it with a quickness.
Charlotte went and fetched the blade.
Once more we all gathered to show that we had spirit
but when we opened up the rabbit, the sun barreled out—
and now with even more new radiant action!
So that's when we cut off the head
of the sun, held it high for all to see.
And ever since then we've been taking our turns,
hoisting it aloft and wearing it
over our own heads. Pools of blood
have formed all over town
but now when things are weird
we don't notice.

POISON IN MY BODY'S FAT

Poison in my body's fat
But where are all the people
I doze all morning dreaming
of records I've listened to
a thousand times   The killdeer
swirl in the back-to-school skies
I look them up on a map,
switching off all intelligence
So instead of brainy neurons firing
up the room, Ohio feels today
the way it always does—Romantic
both coming and going,
which could be the end of all
things, but it's not   I would
like to be running, but I am not
Hurt my hip and that's not cool
Sitting and sweating
this attempt at an anthem
I should never drink again
for as long as I live, and
I should write the longest
monologue of my life
about what it's like to be

both sick and in love with love
like everybody else
who means anything to me
They've got their hearts
out on paper, and they're
waiting for a hammer,
but they're already tender
and if anybody doesn't like it
they can get with being
a better person pretty damn quick
or die fucking-up with their head
in my pocket   The clouds
aren't made of money,
and they aren't made in the USA
either   They aren't made at all
They form and girls like to look
at them, and I like to look at girls,
because it's easier than looking
at clouds   their bra straps
shining out beyond their tanktops
Meanwhile the opportunity
presents itself to look
at something else, the shadow
of a rabbit breaking into my house,
one blade of grass so much longer
than the others   I finish a letter

I started three weeks ago and mail it
so as not to be lonely
I pick up my daughter from her first
day at kindergarten, and now I need
to ask her all about it, how it went
and what she did, which is why
this is finished even though it's not
finished, even though it's not
anything final

THE FALL OF EVERYBODY

It's hard to hear, "It's hard
to hear," when the duct work keeps speaking
its incredible void   The eyelashes
keep batting   The sleepers
keep sleeping, and none of us
really know how we feel about the sky
It shines its dumb amazement
on our beds, so we hunker down
complaining about the meat
we mostly are/our trajectory:
alone in each body, snuggled up
against a wall   But it's not always
like that   Or at least it doesn't have to be
We are all in this sloppified mess
of brains and blood vessels together
across the sea and right here, right now
in this uncommon pasture   Hello,
dear new friends, let me set
your face on fire with my face on fire
with my wishes that your wishes
don't leave anybody out, that your presence
in this potentially electrifying current
few minutes, or in the rest of your life,

blows itself apart in the service
of coming together differently
in paint and guts, on paper,
your whole voice   the meaning
of meaning and the worms in your heart
how to scream scream scream
to make the old ladies ghosts,
the old men to disintegrate, or
their tongues torn out,
to walk the stupid streets
with your attitude's angles
wondering about angels,
the possibilities spinning on the head
of some buttoned up professor
Even the ants can see you
hiding in the bushes   Don't hide in the bushes
Don't come undone at the seams
unless of course you're in love
and he undoes you or she undoes you
At which point immediately
prepare to be annihilated, both in love
and after

A CLOUD OF DECISIONS TRANSLATES

The most meaningful things never wind up
in a window, but sometimes they do
in the belly of a buzzard or a flagship or a spouse
Presently, I'm so tired of walking into this house
and knowing that it's not my house
and won't be my house for several more days
I need a place to wrest this motorcycle
from chance, which is art, so I lay down
my pillow on the head of a pin,
crushing all the winged things
to powder for the baby pigs
What I mean is: I don't know where I live
and should make amends with Heaven,
not to mention all my friends who ever
rummaged through my backpack
looking for a hangover or some
fog to rub against themselves
I've got plenty of fog   You don't
even really need to ask for it, but
probably should as a matter of empathy
and forgiveness for all the times
I've stolen everything
from your wallets to your phones,

then lost them trying not to
in the couch or the forecaster's
high in the 50s and rain all day
I always take the weather
around me so personally when,
mostly, nothing's such a big deal
that we couldn't just go to a diner
and slam some scrambled eggs,
then look up at the night sky
and wonder

FIXT STAR

The streets don't feel
important   The brooms
don't feel   responsive
The marigolds lift
their faces up, same as the girl
on the swing set's phlox
Look and you will find
me, several signals
in frost   The frost
is not important
The streets don't worry
The brooms don't do anything
But the tattooed man
with the pink umbrella
fixes clouds   He is a cloud
fixer   The clouds
are not important
The tattoos don't feel
significant   They are merely
symbols of the twitters
and fractions of lions
The lions actually are important,
vast and flickering

constellations of water,
some freshly bearded
and ready for the fight
They feel us and they flood us
Their faces conduct us
through dust and tall grasses
and ideas about the universe
Suns forming suns
forming suns
forming suns

BALLADEERING THE HEADLIGHTS

It's a very long car   Always the fauna
outnumber the flora   I pick up
where the drugs leave off   Nobody
has any idea how fucked we really are

To see you now as some kind of lantern
in the windshield is essentially a way
of saying I'm too distracted   Pay
attention   This thesis in aspirin   River-

town Brewing Company   Molasses
and cinnamon, the latter as hard to spell
as Cincinnati, Basquiat, Clare and Lord
Tennyson   When the goddess shows up

with her wings in a wad, I stuff them
in my mouth and wonder what life's like
on a bus with young people who won't quit
texting their fingers long enough

to notice the corn-blue landscape,
the mewling of the cat too fat

to chase the string   If this is all
that's left to sing, then perhaps I should

start walking backwards into the ocean
and keep going until I reach
the lost city of crockery, the giant fact
of the Kraken   I will hold your hands

until I can't hold your hands   Or maybe
instead, you can lose me in the trees,
the really tall trees   We'll walk a long time,
and then we'll come to a road

The impact will teach me
to love you

NEGATIVE CAPABILITY

Most days are all the days
we have, which isn't deep
as a lake, it's stupid
as a newspaper   I wear

in my hair a lot of lightning
and girl scouts   You go
to work with a face

on your dashboard   Tonight,
this afternoon, this morning,
the feathers leaking out
from underneath

the coffee maker make me think
that sometimes gravity
cannot be defied

and anyway the rollercoaster
is tired, so it would be
an excellent time
to stand with the telephone poles

for a ridiculously long time
and maybe every once in a while
we could touch

each other's motorbikes
and consider some general
instructions   You need to do
whatever it is you need to do

And I need to not be
such a series of traffic violations
but it's a lot colder today,

so my metal's overwhelming
I can't be expected to read a story
and bring up a couple of beers
from the basement

at exactly the same time   Nobody
can be in two cities at once
Standing in my yard I see

a red-yellow jet emerge
from the leaves of a red-yellow
tree without any irritable reaching
after fact or reason

PLAN A PLAN B

A

made so much sense in the dark,
but now flies from me in the light
of your audience   Or now it trees
through me in the face of your
audience, your audaciousness
to thwart my best efforts to blueprint
this motion for forgiveness
of the whole human racket
So the governor and his devil
make a bet in several languages,
but possibly only implicitly
to gather intelligence, body odor,
dictatorship   Now, doubting everything,
you can call me Rooster, singing
the houses so deliberately and windy,
where two blocks away
a neighbor on the watch list
spots a lonely wolf,
just passing through us,
the backyards and fences,
down to old Kentucky

from Canadian geese
My godhead sends a picture
of your audience
working hard not to rile up
his acquaintance, as if the blue—
which is sky, or the anger, or the beauty
or the weariness all through us—
ever actually exists
A rainbow's a real thing,
my daughter Agnes insists, but not
in the way it is really, so we remind her
in the first place she is six,
and in the second
not to ride her bike through the middle
of a story   She doesn't
remember the conversations
about things both miniscule
and sorry, but she does in her sleep
dream the beginnings and endings
of fairies, which doesn't mean
she still doesn't want one
for her very own, its magic blowing
literally the wind chimes, the wobbled
porch swing swinging low
And all across the city
holding hands and other things,

friends together swaying
more than ever   I want this
to end, or I want it to end never
The cynical people on their heads
without their hands can keep
their balance if they can, but no
they can't   And I am all
a whiteness and a gelatin print
black dress upon a mannequin
in your windows,
though also I am hammered
to a blankness with a flower, a beer
or a horse or a desk in my throat
And meanwhile, the empty heart
of your audience has packed a blanket,
so gets it out, and all of us stay
warm when we visit North Korea
or logorrhea or North-North
of Northness, and sometimes we have
a picnic or instead we find ourselves
at the awful dreamy house
where we meet ourselves, walking in
and walking out, both coming
and going in a shambles to the shambles
There's a sloppiness upon us, as we blink
through comma's coma and the whale

winks out by the light of its own oil
Truly I love talking to you,
my self-inflicted punchbowl,
which I know sounds worse than I mean it
when you mean it   Clearly, you have a way
about town, a waywardness
if anyone does   And this rescue attempt
is littered with stars, fragments
of goats and cooks in boats,
my fogged-out wheelbarrow
so warm and capable
it almost works even covered
in furs   Earnest and grasping,
I get a little nervous
Your audience applauds
You slip through my claws

B

has to be an entirely different creature.
When Dave called me out of the blue
and said, "Man, last night I had a dream
about you reading this poem called

Plan A Plan B," I knew immediately
I had to write the poem and deploy it
in the world somewhere, because

Dave's a prophet. But of course, I also knew,
even before I started, that I'd need a Plan B,
not just because of the poem's title,
but because Plan A, which was to

simply sit down and bust the whole thing out,
would never work, and didn't, since that's what
I always do—jump into the lifeboat and see

where it takes me, but this had to be something
else, and "your audience" kept bothering me,

until eventually "you" slipped through my fingers,
and that's when I knew it was time to enact Plan B,

even though when I read Plan A to Jen
over the phone, she said, "I think that's
my favorite appearance of Agnes

in one of your poems," which made me
feel good, since Jen's read a lot of my poems,
and is a tough critic—though, for what it's worth,
the thing about Plan A that I was most

excited about was the appearance
of the wolf in my neighborhood,
which really happened a few weeks back.

One of our neighbors looked out
her kitchen window, and there it was,
so she took a picture with her phone
and out it went, all over Westwood.

I can only hope the wolf made it safely
to Kentucky, its bluegrass and bourbon,
where even in winter it's warmer than it is

in Canada and probably also North Korea,
though I sort of hate how it imposed itself
in Plan A. I didn't plan that. Nor
did I really plan any of this,

which is one of my poetic problems.
I don't write poems to articulate
some preconceived version of the world.

I write poems to figure out how I see
the world. Thus, making a plan is not
only a drag, it's not even possible.
And while, sadly, Plan A did end up being a failure

(as it never really took off the way I wanted),
Plan B thus far seems a struggling thing, too.
And yet, I wonder if somehow this is actually the poem

that I read in Dave's dream? He seemed to think
there was really something to it, like I'd set
myself on fire with a red-tailed hawk
and the whole congregation sang

"The Old Rugged Cross," our lives
crashing hard into mean electric fences

TRIM BLACK SHIPWRECK

Now turning some weird
middle of nowhere leaf
toward shore,
I will finally be able to tell you
what I've been wanting
to tell you for some time—
that this is not
like the other trips out
to pick up a few things
we need from the store:
dog food and a rake,
some apple wood smoked bacon
Maybe you've noticed my absence
Ten thousand years, possibly more
Can you see it in my armor
I can see it when your shirt gaps
open to a sheer black bra,
p.652, Book XI
Water water everywhere
And monsters
And giants   Sides
of meat and heady wine
Even now, your mouth

Thick splinter in my mind
My body moves its wings to die
but my tears have given up
even flowing   And yet,
great mystery, the curse
now is broken
Last night
I dreamed that a little boy leaned
over an immaculate garden,
teeming with rabbits
and absurd looking blossoms
He seemed in full reverie
as he studied it carefully
He seemed not to know
or not to care
that I was watching
And then all at once I was the boy
glorious and beaming
The two of us were one of us
And then, as if it were a carnival game
we'd played a hundred times,
we reached in among the flowers
and pulled out
the smallest elephant
I have ever seen
in any room in my life

Suddenly it was clear
that anything is possible,
even this Whirlpool
washer and dryer, the sky
with its hand on your hip
gently plying,
and a voice so welcoming
and gentle and sure,
calling me, *Sinner,*
come home

/

POEM FOR GOOD

The sky super-crushed or every grass blade
      humming   These verses all
           cursory   These verses
all the world to me
Somehow they make me feel better
          with wild looks into mailboxes
      or into deadly history, which is nothing
          to be afraid of really, only
      we're all going someday into the eagle's beak
          or over the cliff edge or
off to bed in our warm clothes forever

I've set my sights on getting higher than expected
      tonight   I think the light weighs
          about the same as a racetrack
I go to the wall to make it dimmer
          And with nothing left to undo,
    I imagine being stranger to you
        than ever   O after and after
    all that's happened so radioactively politically,
      I almost can't bear how apart from you
    the moon beams, and I stand on my face to enjoy it

feeling hyperbolic about my fantasies
of kissing every person I see
and all the dead poets
on their faces

In current events, there are uprisings
everywhere, and on Wall Street
money
floods out of the windows
Everyone goes crazy
with a dull green headache
Overwhelming mouths of leaves, or too much
Leaves of Grass for me
for one evening
And yet, it's not enough   The sorry dictator begging
the question before they end him
"Do you not know the difference
between right and wrong?"

Will my own head ever be forgiven
for its dreams?   Will I continue to command
the wildest rides
I have to offer?   The moment is coming
I don't think I can fix it   I just want to be
a good man

I am not desperate, but in the act
of all my poems, wrapped in music,
                    and not a whiff of reason

When I see you, I will smother you in fits
                    to last forever   I will walk
                              into my house
                                        and feel okay

ACKNOWLEDGMENTS, NOTES, AND THANKS

Many thanks to the editors of the following journals where many of these poems, sometimes with different titles or in radically different versions, first appeared: *The Academy of American Poets/poets.org, American Books/Steck Editions, The American Reader, Barn Owl Review, Big Bell, Black Tongue Review, Columbia Poetry Review, Diode Poetry, The Fiddleback, The Greensboro Review, iO: A Journal of New American Poetry, Leveler, Likestarlings, Loaded Bicycle, ONandOnScreen, Pinwheel, Sixth Finch, Sprung Formal* and *Trigger*.

Thanks to Hell Yes Press for including an earlier version of "Poem for Good" in their *21 Love Poems* cassette anthology.

Thanks to Sivan Butler-Rotholz for including "Daily Chores" in the Saturday Poetry Series at the *As It Ought to Be* blog.

"The Power Is Wrong" was written in conjunction with the CS13 Gallery exhibition *Hail Satan: Contemporary Writing and Art from Hell*. A hand-typed version of the poem (including mistakes) also appeared in *Blue Jay Slayer*, published by Aurore Press.

"In Love with the Sound" takes its title from the title of a song by The Saddest Landscape.

"Blasted in the Soft Azure Mountains" was made using a five-color paint swatch from Home Depot. The colors were Soft Azure, Ship-Shape, Mayflower Blue, Fountain Mist, and Pacific Pearl.

MATT HART is the author of seven previous books of poems, including most recently *Everything Breaking / For Good* (YesYes Books, 2019), *Radiant Action* and *Radiant Companion*. Additionally, his poems, reviews, and essays have appeared or are forthcoming in numerous print and online journals, including *The Academy of American Poets* online, *Big Bell, Cincinnati Review, Coldfront, Columbia Poetry Review, Harvard Review, Jam Tarts Magazine, jubilat, Kenyon Review* online, *Lungfull!,* and *POETRY Magazine*, among others. His awards include a Pushcart Prize, a 2013 individual artist grant from The Shifting Foundation, and fellowships from both the Bread Loaf Writers' Conference and the Warren Wilson College MFA Program for Writers. A co-founder and the editor-in-chief of *Forklift, Ohio: A Journal of Poetry, Cooking & Light Industrial Safety*, he lives in Cincinnati where he teaches at the Art Academy of Cincinnati and plays in the band NEVERNEW.

ALSO FROM YESYES BOOKS

Pelican by Emily O'Neill

The Youngest Butcher in Illinois by Robert Ostrom

A New Language for Falling Out of Love by Meghan Privitello

I'm So Fine: A List of Famous Men & What I Had On
    by Khadijah Queen

American Barricade by Danniel Schoonebeek

The Anatomist by Taryn Schwilling

Gilt by Raena Shirali

Panic Attack, USA by Nate Slawson

[insert] boy by Danez Smith

Man vs Sky by Corey Zeller

The Bones of Us by J. Bradley
    [Art by Adam Scott Mazer]

CHAPBOOK COLLECTIONS

Vinyl 45s

    After by Fatimah Asghar

    Inside My Electric City by Caylin Capra-Thomas

    Dream with a Glass Chamber by Aricka Foreman

    Exit Pastoral by Aidan Forster

    Pepper Girl by Jonterri Gadson

    Of Darkness and Tumbling by Mónica Gomery

    Bad Star by Rebecca Hazelton

    Makeshift Cathedral by Peter LaBerge

    Still, the Shore by Keith Leonard

Please Don't Leave Me Scarlett Johansson by Thomas Patrick Levy

Juned by Jenn Marie Nunes

A History of Flamboyance by Justin Phillip Reed

Unmonstrous by John Allen Taylor

Giantess by Emily Vizzo

No by Ocean Vuong

This American Ghost by Michael Wasson

Blue Note Editions

Beastgirl & Other Origin Myths by Elizabeth Acevedo

Kissing Caskets by Mahogany L. Browne

One Above One Below: Positions & Lamentations
     by Gala Mukomolova

Companion Series

Inadequate Grave by Brandon Courtney

The Rest of the Body by Jay Deshpande